Spilling the Beans on...

Napoleon

Bonaparte and his counterparts

Miles Kelly
PUBLISHING

First published in 2000 by Miles Kelly Publishing,
Bardfield Centre, Great Bardfield, Essex CM7 4SL

Reprinted 2001

Printed in Italy

ISBN 1-902947-42-8

2468109753

Cover design and illustration: Inc
Layout design: Gardner Quainton
Art Direction: Clare Sleven

:Spilling the Beans on...

Napoleon

Bonaparte and his counterparts

le shoe shop

le Wellingtons
F.2.00

by Mick Gowar

Illustrations   Mike Mosedale

About the Author

Mick Gowar has written or edited over 40 books for children, including collections of poetry, novels, graphic novels, picture books and short stories. He has visited over 600 schools, libraries, colleges and other venues to give talks and performances of his work, or to lead workshops. As well as writing and performing, he is at present a part-time lecturer in the Department of Illustration and Graphic Arts at Anglia University, Cambridge.

Contents

Chapter 1   Boney'll Get You!   7

Chapter 2   The Rich Get Rich and the
             Poor Get Nothing   19

Chapter 3   The King Must Die   31

Chapter 4   A Gentlemanly Occupation   43

Chapter 5   Brilliant Soldier – Brilliant Organiser   51

Chapter 6   Kill Napoleon   71

Chapter 7   The End of the Empire   83

             Not the End   94

Chapter 1

Boney'll Get You!

I once met a very old man, who told me that when he was a very young boy his grandmother used to tell him that if he didn't go to sleep, or eat his greens, or do as he was told: "Boney'll get you!"

This "Boney" she threatened him with, this bogey man which used to terrify him, (and which she was probably terrified with as a young girl), was Napoleon Bonaparte.

Nowadays Napoleon isn't some monster used to scare children, but most British people still don't know much about the real Napoleon Bonaparte.

Here are some ideas about Napoleon:

He was very short.

Not true: he was 5'6½" (172 cm) tall – average for a Frenchman of his time. The rumour that he was only 5'2" (158 cm) comes from a mistranslation of the old French measurements which were different to the British ones.

He was a ruthless dictator who only cared about personal power, a tyrant like Hitler or Stalin.
Not true: he tried to bring fair laws and equal rights to the people of France and the Empire.

He once said: "Not tonight, Josephine!"
Not true: that line "Not tonight, Josephine" came from a popular English comic song of the early twentieth century.

He died of arsenic poisoning.
Not true: at least as far as the autopsy results are concerned. When his body was examined, a large tumour – a cancer – was found in his stomach. His father also died of stomach cancer.

This book is about the real Napoleon, not the bogey-man.

An Island For Sale

Europe at the end of the eighteenth century, when Napoleon was born, was not made up of the nation states we know today. For example, there was no Italy, no Germany, no Belgium, no Hungary, no Czech or Slovak republics.

Most of Europe and the Middle East was ruled by three huge Empires: the Austrian (or Holy Roman) Empire; the Russian Empire and the Turkish (or Ottoman) Empire.

Italy was mostly divided between the Austrian Empire and the Pope, who was not just a religious leader but also one of the richest and most powerful princes in Europe. A few Italian cities were tiny countries in their own right. All the people spoke the Italian language, but there was no single country called Italy.

Napoleon's parents, Carlo and Letizia Bonaparte, were Italians living on the Mediterranean island of Corsica. Until just before Napoleon's birth, Corsica was ruled from the Italian town of Genoa. Napoleon's father, Carlo, was a nobleman, a lawyer and a fighter for Corsican independence.

Carlo Bonaparte was a friend and supporter of a Corsican rebel leader called Pasquale Paoli. Together they raised an army of Corsican rebels to fight the Genoese. Eventually, the Genoese decided to leave Corsica because of all the trouble caused by the rebel fighters.

This was what Paoli and Carlo had been hoping for. But they assumed the Genoese would just leave and let them run the whole island. The Genoese did not. This is what they did...

For Sale

Delightful Mediterranean Island

Complete with olive groves, fishing ports and peasant farms.

They sold Corsica to the King of France.

Free Corsica!

In 1768, the year before Napoleon was born, the French king took over his new island. Over the next two years, more than 30,000 French soldiers were stationed in Corsica. The Corsican rebels fought bravely, but they were outnumbered by French troops. Paoli, Carlo Bonaparte and the rebel army eventually surrendered to the French.

Excellent opportunities for boar and partridge shooting. Plenty of pine trees and chestnut trees. All mod. cons. including mountains, cold running water and rebel fighters. Would suit large European nation with plenty of soldiers. One Careful Owner.

APPLY: GENOA

The rebels signed a peace treaty with the French. Paoli was allowed to leave the island to live in exile in England. He tried to persuade Carlo and his family to come with him. But Carlo had one baby son, Joseph, and his wife Letizia was pregnant with another child. Carlo and Letizia decided to stay in Corsica. Later that year Napoleon was born, a French citizen because Corsica was now part of France.

 But if Carlo had gone with Paoli, then Napoleon – France's greatest general – would have been born English.

Napoleon's childhood

Although he was born a French citizen, for the first ten years of his life Napoleon didn't speak or write a single word of French. Like all the other children on the island he was brought up speaking and writing Italian.

Carlo hoped that his sons would become lawyers. But education cost a lot of money, and money was something that Carlo and Letizia didn't have.

Then a friend told them about a special scholarship scheme run by the French government to pay for the education of the children of hard-up nobles – which was what Carlo and Letizia were. The only problem was that there were only two types of education offered under the scholarship: to train to become either a priest or a soldier.

It was too good an opportunity to miss, but should their two boys be priests or soldiers? Carlo and Letizia talked it over. Joseph was clever, dreamy and gentle. He wouldn't be much good as a soldier, but he might make an excellent priest.

But what about Napoleon? He was quick and clever, which a good priest should be. But he was also tough, proud and stubborn. Even though he was younger and smaller than Joseph, Napoleon would always beat him if the two boys fought. Although it would mean sending the boys to different schools, Carlo and Letizia decided that Napoleon would have to be trained to be a soldier.

So, in December 1778, Napoleon and Joseph, accompanied by Carlo, boarded the boat for France.

Carlo took the boys to a small town in southern France called Autun. Here they would learn French at the local school before going their separate ways – Joseph to the seminary to learn to be a priest, and Napoleon to the military school in Brienne. On New Year's Day 1779, Carlo said good-bye to the boys and caught the boat back to Corsica.

Napoleon's schooldays

The military school in Brienne which Napoleon went to was a strict school. The boys wore army-style uniforms and slept in little wooden cubicles which were locked at night (they did have chamber pots in their cubicles, just in case).

Remember this is better than any old fairy story!

WORLD HISTORY by A FRENCH MONK

Although it was a military school, all the teachers were monks. The boys were taught all the things that army officers would need to know such as maths, geography (especially map-making), and how to build fortifications.

They were also taught to be very patriotic. The monks taught the boys that France was the greatest country in the world, with the bravest army and the wisest king. The monks were so concerned to make the boys love their country that they sometimes told lies (not something monks are supposed to do). For example, in history lessons the boys were taught that:

 Germany had once been part of the French Empire.

 In the battles of Agincourt and Crécy the army of the French king had been defeated by French rebels (NOT the English army).

Germany France had never – repeat NEVER – lost a battle to the English.

16

The days in the school were very long indeed. This is the actual timetable for a typical day at the school when Napoleon was a pupil:

6.00 am: Sleeping cubicles unlocked and cadets woken. Cadets wash and put on uniform.

6.30 am: Class has early morning "pep" talk – similar to a class assembly – usually on French law and the importance of good behaviour.

7.00 am: Mass.

7.30 am: Breakfast: bread, fruit and a glass of water.

8.00 - 10.00 am: Lessons in the usual school subjects: Latin, history, geography, maths and physics.

10.00am -12.00: Lessons in military subjects: how to build fortifications, drawing and colouring maps.

12.00: Lunch (main meal of the day): soup, boiled meat, another meat or fish dish, dessert, and a glass of red wine mixed with water.

1.00 pm: Recreation.

2.00 - 4.00 pm: More lessons in Latin, history, geography etc.

4.00 - 6.00 pm: Lessons in either fencing, dancing, gymnastics, music or a foreign language (either German or English) depending on the day.

6.00 - 8.00 pm: Homework.

8.00 pm: Supper: roast, a second meat or fish dish, and a salad.

9.00 - 10.00 pm: Recreation.

10.00 pm: Evening prayers and lights out.

Napoleon stayed at the military school for five years. This is his school report for his last year:

> He is very regular in his conduct and has always distinguished himself by his interest in mathematics. He has a sound knowledge of history and geography. He is very poor at dancing and drawing. He will make an excellent sailor.

What isn't mentioned in the report is Napoleon's worst subject: spelling. It was awful – probably because he hadn't learnt French until he was nearly ten years old. For the rest of his life, Napoleon misspelt even very simple French words and often mispronounced them too.

What might come as a surprise, though, is the last sentence of the report. At this time, the boy who would grow up to be France's greatest general wanted to be a naval officer.

Napoleon wrote a letter asking to join the navy. Possibly the letter got lost or maybe no-one bothered to reply, but when he got no answer Napoleon applied to the Military Academy in Paris to be trained as an artillery officer. This time he was accepted.

Chapter 2

The Rich Get Rich and the Poor Get Nothing

Napoleon had been brought up to believe that France was the greatest country in the world, with the best king and the bravest army. Coming to Paris was a great shock for Napoleon, because it was obvious that there were some big problems in France; problems which the monks had never mentioned.

The nobles – the rich lords and ladies – and the royal family lived in incredible luxury, while the poorest people starved in the streets.

Unlike Britain, France was ruled under the old, medieval feudal system. This meant that all the land was owned by rich nobles – lords, dukes and counts. Poor farmers – the peasants – had to pay the rich lords to farm the land. There were no elections in France and no parliament to make laws. The law was simply what the king said. He was an absolute monarch which meant that he had the absolute right to do whatever he liked.

One of the powers the king had was to send anyone to prison without trial just by writing a *lettre de cachet* – which means a sealed letter. It was a single sheet of paper signed by the king and sealed with wax. The person whose name appeared on the paper would go to prison or be sent into exile for as long as the king wanted. Louis XVI, who was king when

Napoleon was a young man, signed over 14,000 *lettres de cachet* during his reign.

Lettre de Cachet

Go to Jail! Go directly to Jail and don't argue! You won't get a trial, and you'll stay there until I say you can come out.

Signed,

Louis (King)

PS. I don't actually know who you are or anything about you, but one of my ministers said you were bad, dangerous and deserved to be locked up and that's good enough for me.

On their own lands, the nobles had similar powers to a king. French peasants were virtually slaves to the lords who owned the land. Every year the peasants had to give part of their crops to their lord. They also had to work for no money building roads and bridges. French peasants had few possessions and hardly any money; the rich lords owned nearly everything.

There were some the things that the peasants had to do by law and there were some things lords *could* do by law. Work out which ones are True or False.

Peasants had to:

■ work for free for the lord for several days every year
■ pay a tax to their lord every year
■ give part of their crops to their lord every year
■ grind their wheat in their lord's mill and pay for using it
■ bake their bread in an oven owned by their lord and pay for using it
■ crush their grapes in their lord's press and pay for using it
■ pay a tax on anything they took to sell at a market held on the lord's land

Lords could:

■ ride across peasants' fields when hunting, even if there were crops growing
■ keep rabbits, which the peasants weren't allowed to kill even if they were eating their crops
■ keep pigeons, which the peasants weren't allowed to kill even if they were eating their crops
■ ...but, because of all their privileges, the rich lords paid more taxes than the peasants

Got any spare change?

Every one of those statements is true, except for the last one. Believe it or not it, was the peasants – the people with hardly any money – who paid the highest taxes.

And not only did they pay taxes to the king, they also had to give one-tenth of all their income or the crops they grew to the church. All the senior churchmen, such as the bishops and the cardinals, came from the wealthiest families. Like the nobles, the rich clergy also paid virtually no taxes.

You don't have to be a financial genius to work out that any country that depends for its money on taxing people with hardly any money is heading for disaster.

Revolution!

By 1789, Napoleon had left the military academy and was an artillery officer in the small garrison town of Valence in the south of France. French officers in those days were allowed to choose where they served, and Napoleon chose Valence because it was the closest garrison to Corsica. His father had died, and although he wasn't the oldest, the rest of the family looked to Napoleon to take over from Carlo as head of the family.

Napoleon and Joseph now had six younger brothers or sisters who all needed educating, clothing and feeding. Food was getting more and more expensive. Napoleon did his best help. He sent as much of his pay as he could home to his mother to help pay for the large family, but Napoleon's mother was struggling.

But families poorer than the Bonapartes were facing real hunger. In the summer of the year before, freak hailstorms had badly damaged the crops before they were harvested. Then the winter had been the worst anyone could remember – rivers and lakes had frozen for months. When the thaw came, the roads had flooded. What little food had been saved from the hail and ice couldn't get into the towns because of the floods. The price of bread rocketed. The poor people in cities such as Paris began to starve.

For years the ordinary people – the workers in the town as well as the peasants in the countryside – had been angry about the large amount of taxes they had to pay compared to the tiny amounts paid by the rich nobles. They were angry too about the privileges of the nobles, and they were angry about the *lettres de cachet*. The shortage of food was the final straw.

In the summer of 1789 the people of France turned to violence to get what they wanted. In Paris, an angry mob destroyed the Bastille prison, and in the country gangs of starving peasants attacked and burnt the houses of their rich landlords, often with the rich landlords still inside.

King Louis tried to control the growing revolution. He summoned the ancient French council – the Estates General – to meet at the Royal Palace of Versailles to suggest reforms. The Estates General renamed themselves the National Assembly and tried to become a proper parliament and rule France like the British parliament ruled Britain – passing laws to abolish the old feudal rights of the nobles. But changes didn't come quickly enough for the poorest people in Paris.

In October, a crowd of women demanding bread, marched from Paris to the Royal Palace at Versailles. When she heard what they wanted, Queen Marie Antoinette was supposed to have said:

"If they have no bread, then let them eat cake!"

But she didn't say this. It had been said, but by Queen Marie Thérèse, the wife of Louis XIV, a hundred years earlier.

A riotous crowd broke into the palace, and forced the king and queen to come back to Paris and live in the Tuileries Palace instead of Versailles. The revolution was getting beyond the control of the politicians in the National Assembly.

Napoleon the Revolutionary

Far away from Paris, in the garrison town of Valence, news reached Napoleon and the other soldiers of the revolution in Paris.

Napoleon, the son of a freedom fighter, was an enthusiastic supporter of the Revolution. Although his parents had been nobles, Napoleon believed passionately in the principles of the Revolution: *Liberté, Egalité, Fraternité* – Freedom, Equality and Brotherhood. That meant: freedom for the ordinary people from unjust taxes and the feudal payments to lords; equality for everyone – the same laws for all; all Frenchmen are brothers – no more divisions into nobles and peasants.

Napoleon organised a club of pro-revolutionaries – a sort of political supporters' club. When the order came to confiscate church land and sell it to the ordinary farmers, Napoleon organised the sale in Valence.

Then in June 1791, the king did something very stupid: he tried to make a run for it.

Louis XVI had pretended to support the revolution, but secretly he'd been hoping that the revolution would collapse and the old ways could come back. Now he saw that wasn't going to happen, he and his family disguised themselves, slipped out of an unguarded door of the Tuileries Palace in the middle of the night, and drove by coach to the Belgian border. The coach was stopped at the town of Varennes, the royal family was recognised and brought back to Paris as prisoners.

Back in Valence, Napoleon made a speech publicly condemning the king's action.

Napoleon realised that many of the most senior officers in the army were still loyal to the king. Along with a number of other junior officers, he campaigned for the creation of a new army, a citizens' army: the National Guard.

In the autumn of 1791, Napoleon was rewarded for his support of the Revolution. He was elected as one of four lieutenant colonels of the Corsican National Guard. He was 22 years old.

War against the Revolution

In March 1792, the old Austrian Emperor, Leopold, died. The new Emperor Francis II, was Queen Marie Antoinette's nephew, and was determined to destroy the French Revolution and rescue his aunt. He and the King of Prussia publicly promised to help Louis and Marie Antoinette. They also called on the other kings of Europe to join them.

The French army attacked first, but the Austrian and Prussian armies were much better organised and equipped.

There were rumours, probably true, that Marie Antoinette sent some of the secret battle plans of the French army to her nephew, who shared them with the Prussians.

The National Assembly gave weapons to all the citizens of Paris so that they could defend themselves. The Prussian army came within a few miles of Paris before being beaten by the French army.

The Paris mob, which was now armed, turned on the king and royal family. Helped by the National Guard, they attacked the Tuileries Palace, killed the king's bodyguard of 600 Swiss soldiers, and took the royal family to the Temple Prison.

Chapter 3

The King Must Die

In September 1792 France was declared a republic – a state without a king. In November the ex-king Louis XVI was tried for High Treason and found guilty. In January 1793 he was executed by guillotine in Paris.

His personal servant stayed with Louis in prison to look after him. This is what he wrote about the day of his master's execution in his diary:

I remained alone in the room, numb with grief. The drums and the trumpets announced that His Majesty had left the prison. An hour later, salvoes of artillery and cries of Long Live The Nation! and Long Live The Republic filled the air. The best of kings was no more!

The execution of the King of France horrified the other monarchs of Europe. Soon Austria and Prussia were joined by Britain, Spain and the Kingdom of Piedmont, in Northern Italy, in their war against France.

The French government set up an emergency committee, called the Committee for Public Safety, which had the power to do anything the 12 members thought necessary to save the Revolution from its enemies.

But although the Committee was popular in Paris, in the west of France thousands of peasants and supporters of the king began an armed rebellion against the government.

It was a revolution against the revolution.

The Reign of Terror

The Committee for Public Safety, led by a lawyer named
Maximilien Robespierre, attempted to put down the revolt by
executing everyone it thought was an enemy of the Republic.

A law was passed called The Law of Suspects. Under this
law every town was to make lists of people thought to be
against the government. In a single year a quarter of a million
people were arrested and nearly 18,000 people were executed.
In Paris more than 3,000 people were executed, including
the queen.

That year was known as the Reign Of Terror.

All the executions were carried out in public, in front of
large crowds which often booed and threw rotting rubbish at
the condemned prisoners as they were driven to the scaffold
on open carts called tumbrels.

The Guillotine

It would have been impossible to execute so many people if
it hadn't been for the guillotine. It was invented by a
Dr Joseph-Ignace Guillotin who tested his new invention on
dead bodies in the hospital at Bicetre. Dr Guillotin kindly

offered the machine to the French Republic as the official means of execution. Unlike a man with an axe, he assured the committee, it could chop off heads all day and never get tired.

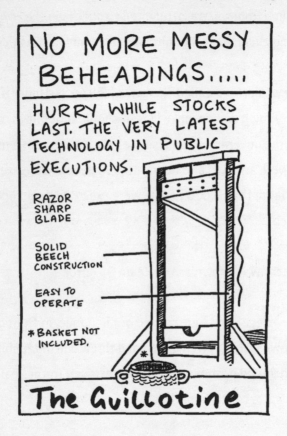

But even the guillotine couldn't execute people fast enough for the authorities in the west of France where the rebellion was strongest. 2,000 captured rebels were executed by being drowned in the river Loire, and in Lyons prisoners were lined up in front of mass graves and shot with cannons.

Napoleon Saves the Revolution

The port of Toulon, in the south of France, was one of the centres of rebellion against the revolution. In August of 1793, the rebel leaders in Toulon declared the dead king's son to be the new king, Louis XVII, and they allowed a fleet of English, Spanish and Italian ships to come into the port and land troops there.

This was very bad news for the government in Paris. They already had more than 800,000 soldiers fighting against the armies of Prussia and Austria. They didn't have the men or weapons to fight another war in the south. This looked like it could be the end of the Revolution.

Just when things started to look really bad Lieutenant Colonel Napoleon Bonaparte volunteered to help fight the invading troops and the rebels in Toulon.

When he arrived, the town was under siege – surrounded by troops loyal to the revolution, but no-one seemed to know what to do next. Because of the shortage of good generals, the army surrounding the town was commanded by a former royal portrait painter, who was then replaced by an ex-dentist who got sick at the sight of blood. The siege was getting nowhere.

Napoleon took control. He led an attack on one of the forts defending the town, and from there organised an artillery attack on the British ships anchored in the port. Faced with a ferocious attack by cannons, the British admiral got the troops back on board and slipped out of port during the night.

But Napoleon had been wounded in the leg leading the attack on the fort. At first, the army doctor wanted to cut off his leg – this was the normal treatment for bad wounds, to stop them getting infected. After another examination, though, he decided to risk not amputating, so Napoleon was left with a deep scar, but two legs.

Napoleon Saves the Revolution Again

Napoleon was the hero of Toulon. As a reward for his services, he was promoted to Brigadier General at the age of only 22. He was also a friend of Augustin Robespierre, brother of the powerful leader of the Committee for Public Safety, Maximilien. Everything seemed be going Napoleon's way.

But no-one in France was safe from accusation, imprisonment and execution. Eventually, having denounced, imprisoned or executed nearly everyone who disagreed with them, the members of the Committee for Public Safety turned on each other. Robespierre himself was executed, with 71 of his closest followers including his brother, Augustin. As a close friend of Augustin, Napoleon was also imprisoned.

Fortunately for Napoleon, the people and the government had had enough of bloodshed. The Committee for Public Safety was disbanded and a new government was formed consisting of a council led by five ministers called Directors.

Napoleon was let out of prison, but no-one in the new government wanted to give him a job. He waited in Paris for a new post. He waited, and he waited.

Although his pay should have been enough to live on, Napoleon was still sending most of his money to his mother, and Paris was the most expensive place to live in the whole of France. When he ran out of money, Napoleon sold his carriage, and moved out of his flat to live in a cheap hotel. He couldn't afford a new uniform when his old one started to wear out, and had to walk around Paris looking like a tramp. He even gave up wearing gloves as (he said) "a useless expense."

Then one night, Napoleon decided as a rare treat to cheer himself up that he'd go to see a play – in one of the cheapest seats, of course. Walking to the theatre, he saw some National Guardsmen shouting anti-government slogans and gathering together an armed mob.

Napoleon went at once to the parliament building. Some representatives were panicking, and nobody seemed to know what to do. Napoleon offered to help.

Once again he used artillery guns, this time to defend the French government from a rebellion by the Paris mob. Once again he won, and once again he was a hero.

In Command

This time Napoleon got the reward he thought he deserved. He was put in command of the Army of the Alps. His job was to beat the Austrian army and their allies in Northern Italy.

Like many soldiers about to go to war, Napoleon quickly married his sweetheart, a widow with two children whose first husband had been executed during the Terror.

On March 9th, 1796, General Napoleon Bonaparte married Josephine Beauharnais, and two days later, on March 11, he took up his new command. And all through the coming war, whenever there was a break in the fighting, Napoleon would take out a small framed picture of Josephine which he carried everywhere with him, show it to anyone who was nearby, and then tell them what a wonderful wife Josephine was. Then he would kiss the picture passionately and put it back in his pocket.

An Army of Scarecrows

You would imagine that Napoleon would have a crack team of highly-trained soldiers to defeat the might of the Austrians. If

Napoleon had the same thought he was in for a shock. The army with which Napoleon was supposed to beat the Austrians in Italy was described by one of his fellow officers as "an army of scarecrows". That was far too complimentary.

None of the soldiers had real uniforms. Some of the older soldiers were still wearing the rags that were all that was left from their pre-revolutionary uniforms. Most wore whatever clothes they owned. Only a few had proper boots, and most of the soldiers either tied rags round their feet or wore homemade flip-flops made from plaited straw. They hadn't been paid for months and hadn't eaten in days.

Napoleon had been given a little money to pay for the war. He spent it all in the first few days. He bought 18,000 pairs of boots and enough corn to make three months supply of bread – but only if the soldiers mixed their flour with ground chestnuts.

But worse than the state of their boots or their rations were their weapons. They were old-fashioned to the point of being useless. The best equipped soldiers had old-fashioned muskets. These were the same sort the French army had been using for over a hundred years. Gunpowder and shot had to be poured down the barrel and pushed in with a ramrod. A soldier might be able to fire two rounds a minute, if he was a crack shot. But after about 20 minutes, he would have to stop – in the middle of a battle – and clean his musket.

But there was nothing Napoleon could do about the muskets. The army would just have to make do. If they won – and it was a big **if** – it wouldn't be because of their equipment; they would have to use what little they had very cleverly. It would take a lot of luck and some very cunning tactics.

Chapter 4

A Gentlemanly Occupation

The old rules of war, like the old rules of government, came from the Middle Ages. They were based on the old chivalric idea that war was a game for gentlemen, and no-one got hurt – except the peasant foot-soldiers, and they didn't count.

Most battles until Napoleon's time went like this:

Two armies marched towards each other until they reached a place where both agreed they would have a battle – this was often done by the opposing commanders meeting each other for a friendly chat a day or two before the battle.

Both armies got ready – sharpened their swords etc. This could take some time.

 They faced each other on flat ground.

 They lined up in two long straight lines.

 When everyone was ready they marched towards each other – in step.

 They fought for a few hours.

 Both sides went back to their tents.

 Result: usually a draw.

If Napoleon had fought by the old rules he would have lost. So he broke all those rules:

 He attacked the enemy before they had a chance to get ready.

 He attacked anywhere – not just on flat ground.

 He attacked from any direction – from the front, from the sides, from the back.

 He didn't give a fig for what was "gentlemanly" – he attacked where the enemy looked weakest.

 He moved his troops incredibly quickly – attacking, winning, marching on again, then attacking again.

 He insisted on discipline in his army – he did his best to stop his soldiers looting (stealing from civilians).

 He demanded and got sole command of his army – he didn't like sharing.

Napoleon and his army of scarecrows thrashed the Austrian army – to the delight of the ordinary Italian people. They were delighted because not only did Napoleon drive out the Austrians from the north of Italy, but he also set up a new republic in the north of Italy based on the French Republic. That meant the old feudal rights of the nobles were abolished and there was a new fairer system of laws and taxes.

To Egypt

The Directors were so pleased with Napoleon's success in Italy that they promoted him again. He was made commander of the army to invade Britain.

Napoleon went to the channel coast to look at his troops. He was very keen to start the invasion as soon as possible, but what he saw made him call the invasion off. Most of the troops were badly-equipped young recruits, the weather in the channel was appalling – gales and driving rain – and the boats for the invasion were poorly-built and leaky. If they tried to cross the channel, the British navy would easily destroy any ship that wasn't already sinking. Napoleon decided on another way to attack Britain – by going east.

Much of Britain's wealth depended on trade with the East, and in particular bringing to Europe crops and goods from India, which had recently become part of the British Empire. Napoleon decided to invade Egypt, which was part of the Turkish Empire. Then, if the invasion of Egypt was successful, he could march even further East – maybe even attack India itself.

Everything went well for Napoleon to start with. The French quickly defeated the Turkish army in a great battle fought near the pyramids. (Some people say that it was a French gunner in that battle who accidentally blew the nose off the Sphinx.)

But Napoleon hadn't come to Egypt just to fight. He'd also come to explore and learn. He brought with him scientists and scholars as well as soldiers.

Cracking a Code

Like many Europeans of the time, Napoleon was fascinated by the remains of ancient Egypt – the pyramids, the temples, the paintings and sculptures, and especially the strange picture writing or hieroglyphics. At that time, no-one knew how to read hieroglyphics. One of the scientists, a man named

Tancret, made a great discovery. He found a black stone near a town called Rosetta which had three different types of writing on it. One text was in ancient Greek, one in modern Egyptian and the third was in hieroglyphics. Tancret realised that the texts in modern Egyptian and ancient Greek were the same. So the hieroglyphics were almost certainly the same. He found, by comparing the three pieces of writing, that he could make out a name: Ptolemy. The texts were the same! What had been discovered was the key to the hieroglyphic code. It was a triumph for all the historians and scientists.

But the military side of the expedition had turned into a disaster. All the ships that had brought Napoleon's army to Egypt were anchored offshore near an Egyptian port called Aboukir. A British fleet commanded by Nelson found the French ships, surrounded them and sunk them. Napoleon's army was now stranded. They couldn't get back to France; they couldn't reach India.

For a year, Napoleon and his army were stuck in Egypt. They defeated the Turkish army again and set up a French-style republic for the Egyptian people to rule themselves. Then, in the summer of 1799, four French ships got through. On board one of the ships was a packet of two-week old French newspapers. Eagerly, Napoleon started to read the news from home.

The news was terrible.

La Poste en Dimanche

BIG SET-BACK FOR REVOLUTION:
Western France in Rebel Hands

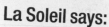

La Soleil says:

Dump the dodgy Directors!

Bring Back The king!

Long Live Louis XVIII!

See page 3 for exclusive pics of Marie Antoinette, painted before she died!

Le Télégraphe

FRANCE AT WAR WITH BRITAIN, AUSTRIA, PRUSSIA, TURKEY & SICILY – and losing!

Napoleon had saved the republic twice before. He was certain that he was the only person who could save it now. He took the four ships, and with a few friends and senior officers, returned at once to France leaving the rest of his army still stranded in Egypt.

It took another two years before Napoleon could arrange to get what was left of his Egyptian army back to France.

I'm in charge

When Napoleon returned to France in 1799 he found things were as bad as the newspapers said. Napoleon at once organised a conspiracy to seize power, helped by his brother Lucien, who was already one of the five Directors.

The brothers went to the government council and told the deputies that rebels were about to attack and capture Paris. The only way to stop the rebels, the brothers said, was to put Napoleon – who had already saved the Revolution twice – in charge of all the troops in Paris. They also said that it was much too dangerous for the council to stay in Paris, they should go somewhere safer. **All this was a complete lie.**

The council members got out of Paris as fast as they could. They set up a new meeting place in the village of St Cloud, just outside Paris. But by the time Napoleon went to see them again the next day, the council members had found out that the story of the rebellion was a great big trick. They were furious.

This, according to the official record of the council, is what happened when Napoleon came into the council chamber:

DEPUTIES (rushing forward trying to grab Napoleon): *Tyrant! Dictator!*

OTHER DEPUTIES (waving pistols and knives): *Kill him!*

SOLDIERS (outside): *Listen to that noise! The general's in danger! Quick! We've got to save him!*

Soldiers rush into the chamber. Surround Napoleon to keep deputies away.

Deputies seeing soldiers panic. One soldier gets stabbed in the arm protecting Napoleon.

DEPUTIES: *They've come to kill us all!*

Several deputies jump out of the window.

DEPUTY: *I'm getting out of here!*

A few deputies stayed. Those that stayed voted to form a new kind of government with Napoleon in charge.

It was to be a government of three Consuls – an idea Napoleon got from reading about the ancient Roman Republic – with himself as First Consul.

Napoleon organised an election – a referendum – to see whether the people of France approved. 1,500 people voted against the new government, but three million voted in favour. It looked as though Napoleon was the people's choice, but in reality he was now the military dictator of France.

Chapter 5

Brilliant Soldier –
Brilliant Organiser

Napoleon's first job as Consul was to defend France against
the armies of the coalition – Austria, Britain, Sicily, Turkey and
Russia. He needed a big victory which would make his enemies
want a truce rather than continue with the war. Napoleon
decided that the weakest part of the alliance was the Austrian
army in northern Italy. However, the Austrian army was
expecting an attack.

What Napoleon did was the one thing the Austrian's weren't
expecting. Instead of attacking over the border, he marched
his army into Switzerland and over the Alps and attacked the

Austrian army from behind, near a village called Morengo.

The French army won. Later in the year, they beat another Austrian army at the Battle of Hohelinder in Germany.

Just as Napoleon hoped, the Austrians asked for peace and the coalition fell apart. In order to get peace, Austria gave France not only northern Italy, but also Belgium and some German states.

The next year, 1802, Napoleon held another election. This time he asked the French people if he should become Consul for Life. Eight thousand said: "No". However three-and-a-half million said: "Yes". Napoleon was now – in all but name – king.

Now that France was safe from attack, Napoleon began sorting out the messes that had been left behind by the Terror, the rule of the Directors and all the wars.

He found the cleverest accountants, lawyers and thinkers in France to help him and set to work. In five years he completely changed the way France was run in almost every way:

 The law was a complete mess. Every little area of France seemed to have its own laws and customs.

Napoleon, with his advisors, started from scratch and devised a whole new system of laws, called the Napoleonic Code. It's still the basis of French law today.

 He completely changed the education system, opening hundreds of new secondary schools called lycées which were run like the military school he'd gone to at Brienne.

 He introduced a national curriculum that all French schools had to follow, and a school-leaving certificate called the Baccalauréate, which is still the French leaving certificate today.

 He reformed the tax laws, and the system of tax collecting. For the first time in years, taxes actually came to the government instead of disappearing into the pockets of the tax collectors.

 He even made peace with Britain (although it only lasted a year).

Napoleon's clothes

If you'd been living in Paris in, say, 1802 and seen Napoleon you would never have guessed from his clothes that he was dictator of all France.

Most kings, emperors and dictators like to show how important they are by wearing fancy uniforms, covered in medals and decorations. Napoleon was quite the opposite. He didn't like display, or spending money on clothes or fancy living of any sort. He liked plain clothes, and would keep the same clothes for a long time.

He had a particular "uniform" that he always wore:

 A flannel vest and short cotton pants – maybe four or five years old (remember, Napoleon didn't believe in spending money on clothes).

 A plain linen shirt and white silk stockings.

White cashmere breeches, held up by braces.

If in Paris, shoes with small gilt buckles. Napoleon didn't like new shoes, because he had very delicate feet. Whenever he bought a pair of new shoes, he made a servant with the same size feet wear them for two or three days to "break them in" for him.

If he was at home, his favourite footwear were slippers made of soft green or red morrocan leather which he would wear until they fell to pieces.

If he was on campaign, Napoleon wore plain black leather riding boots.

A long white cashmere waist-coat.

A muslin cravat.

The plain green frock coat of a Colonel in the Chasseurs. It had gilt buttons and a scarlet collar, but no lace or embroidery. He usually kept his coats and breeches for up to three years.

A bicorn (two-cornered) hat made of beaver fur. He always wore his hat outdoors, and carried it in his left hand when he was indoors. His hat had another purpose apart from keeping Napoleon's head warm: when he lost his temper, he would often throw his hat on the ground and jump up and down on it.

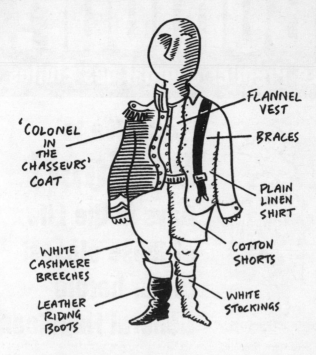

'COLONEL IN THE CHASSEURS' COAT

FLANNEL VEST

BRACES

PLAIN LINEN SHIRT

WHITE CASHMERE BREECHES

COTTON SHORTS

LEATHER RIDING BOOTS

WHITE STOCKINGS

But what was Napoleon really like? He lived at a time before there were celebrity magazines such as *Hello* and *OK*, or tabloid gossip columns. (These persuade members of a famous person's family or people who work for them to give interviews on the celebrity's private life.)

But this is what some of the people who knew Napoleon best might have told a journalist from:

Bonjour!

Le Premier Journal des Étoiles

His valet, Constant

Exclusive to
Bonjour!
Days in the Life of those closest to our heroic General Napoleon

His secretary, Méneval

His chef

THE START OF A TYPICAL DAY

By Napoleon's valet

My name is Constant, and I'm valet to the First Consul, General Napoleon Bonaparte. That means I'm his personal servant, and I look after the General in all matters – and I do mean in all matters. I run his bath, help him dress, and make sure that he has all the little things that a gentleman needs to get him through the day – like his snuff box and perfumed handkerchiefs.

I normally get up just before 5.30 am. After I've dressed, and before I wake the General, I always check that the other servants have lit the log fires in all eight rooms of General and Madame Bonaparte's apartment. As you may know, the General was born on the island of Corsica in the Mediterranean, and he's ever so sensitive to the cold. He likes blazing log fires all year round – summer and winter.

> **"My brains work best at dawn, Constant."**

Then I go and wake him between six and seven o'clock. The General likes to get up early. He often says to me: "My brains work best at dawn, Constant."

The General and Madame have separate rooms – of

61

course – but they always sleep in Madame's room. So I take in his dressing gown – white cotton in

summer and swans' down in winter – and his leather slippers. He loves those slippers! He'll wear a pair until they're falling off his feet in strips.

Then we go up the small staircase to the General's room, where I'll serve him a cup of tea if he wants a hot drink, or a glass of orange-flower flavoured water if he wants something cooling. Then, while I'm running his bath, he'll open his letters and look at the newspapers – but it'll only be a quick glance, because reading the newspapers is my job.

The General loves hot baths – and long ones, too. Usually he'll lie in the bath for an hour – topping it up with hot water – while I sit by the tub reading the newspapers to him. He sometimes has the bath so hot that I can't see to read the newspapers for the thick clouds of steam.

After his bath the General shaves. Now here's an unusual thing – I've known many fine gentlemen in my time, but the General is the only one I've ever come across who always shaves himself! Now you must promise not to tell anyone else what I'm going to tell you: although we're at war with the awful English, the General will only shave with English razors – enemy razors! Always the same ones, with pearl handles made in a place called Birmingham. You mustn't repeat this, but the General says that French steel isn't good enough! Then he'll ask me if I think he's shaved himself close enough. But he always has. I tell you, if things go badly for him in the future, the General could always make a living as a barber!

You'd think the General would be clean enough by now, after having an hour-long bath, wouldn't you? But oh, no. The General's very particular about keeping clean. Now he'll wash his face and neck with soap and wash his hands with almond paste, before cleaning his teeth.

"He's got beautiful white teeth"

He's got beautiful white teeth, has the General. He's got his own dentist, M. Dubois, but he's never needed him. The General always cleans his teeth twice – once with toothpaste, then with powdered coral. Then he'll scrape his tongue with a silver scraper – like the gentleman he is – and finish off with a mouthwash of water and brandy.

Has the General finished his washing? No! Next, he strips to the waist and I have to pour eau-de-Cologne all over his chest and back and scrub him with a stiff bristled brush. Only then is he ready to get dressed. By that time, I feel like I've done a full day's work and it's not even 9 o'clock...

A WORKING DAY

By Napoleon's secretary

…and that's when my working day begins. My name is Méneval, and I am the General's secretary. Constant thinks he works hard, but I say no one works harder than me – except the General, of course. He is an extraordinary man – the work he gets through in a day – and I, being his secretary have to write down every decision, every note, every letter.

> **"My brain works so fast"**

You see, the General dictates everything to me. He's often said to me: "I could never write everything down myself, Méneval. My brain works so fast, my hand could never keep up." My hand can barely keep up – even though I'm taking everything down in shorthand.

Le blah! blah! blah! blah! blah! et blah!

But there's another reason that the General doesn't write – and you must promise not to tell anyone. The General's handwriting is appalling. When he tries to write fast it looks like a spider's fallen in the ink and then run all over

> **"The General's writing is appalling."**

the page. And his spelling – that's even worse than his handwriting! I suppose it's because the General was born on Corsica, and the first language he learnt was Italian. But even that's no excuse for some of the mistakes he makes. The other day he even spelt Madame Bonaparte's family name wrong – as he always does.

We work in his study. It's a lovely room, with huge windows looking over the palace gardens and the River Seine – or so I'm told. I never get to see the view myself. I sit at a desk in front of the window, but with my back to it. And with the speed the General works I'm lucky if I have time to breathe, let alone snatch a glance out of the window.

Many people walk up and down when they dictate. The General marches. Up and down the room, up and down, like a soldier on parade. For eight or ten hours a day! He must walk miles and miles.

But it's an extraordinary experience, listening to him dictate. He never seems to lose the thread of what he's thinking and saying. Other people would lose concentration once in a while and say: "What did I just say, Méneval?" or "Where was I, Méneval?" But the General – never! And he dictates a letter or a note just like he talks. So it's like listening to a conversation. Sometimes I have to look up from my work to make sure that General Murat – or whoever he's writing to – isn't there in the room with us.

He'll take a quick lunch at eleven o'clock, but there's hardly time to write up a fraction of what he's dictated, before we start again. It's a blessing when he has a Council meeting to go to, and then I can catch up on some of the backlog.

And when they day's finished, and I fall into bed exhausted, am I allowed to rest? No! Sometimes he'll wake up in the night and remember something he needs to write urgently. Will he write it out himself? Will he wait until the morning? No. He'll wake me up and off we go again, him striding up and down the study and me taking down dictation at top speed. After a couple of hours, when his throat's dry and my wrist's aching, he'll order a couple of water-ices from the kitchen to refresh us. Then, as soon as we've finished the ices, he's off again.

> **"Why do you work so hard?"**

Once I asked him: "Why do you work so hard?". He just pointed to himself and said: "The ox has been harnessed, and now it must plough."

66

NAPOLEON'S CHEF

They complain – but they are merely servants. Whereas I am a great artist! I am the best chef in the whole of France – which means, of course, I am the best chef in the whole world. So naturally, I am the General's personal chef... and all my skills are wasted!

You see, the General hates luxury. A General who hates luxury and the fine things in life – have you heard of such a thing?

He dresses like an ordinary soldier and eats like a peasant – but please don't tell anyone I said so. Do you

"I am a great artist!"

know what his favourite food is? Go on, guess... Beans and potatoes! And what does he drink with his food – cheap plonk bought from the local grocer!

Now I know we shouldn't talk about the old days – when you-know-who was king – but I used to cook for royalty. Yes, the Duke of Bourbon himself! Now there was a man who appreciated good food, good wine – and a good chef. But the General...

The other week I cooked a dinner – only four courses: soup, grilled fish, chicken fried provençale style, and dessert – that the old Duke would have thought just a light snack between meals.

The General called me in when dinner was finished. (He gobbled it up in less than half an hour, as usual). I was expecting him to say: "Well done.

"And no more garlic!"

Delicious!" But what did the general say? "You've made me eat too much." A wonderful meal and he's annoyed! "From now on, no more than two courses – understand?" I was about to leave, but he called me back. "And no more garlic in the fried chicken. I don't like the taste of garlic."

I didn't know what to say. The ruler of France and he doesn't like the taste of garlic! I said to him, "So what would you like me to cook?"

He looks me straight in the eye – me, the best chef in the whole of France, remember – and says: "Pork sausages."

But the General likes men who speak their mind. So I said to him, straight out: "But that's peasant food, General. If I serve you sausages you'll be up all night with indigestion."

"Sausages," he repeated. "I want you to cook me sausages."

So I did what he asked – well, almost. I couldn't bring myself to cook that revolting pork rubbish, so – quite brilliantly, I thought – I made him the most delicate and delicious sausages from minced partridges. Exquisite! They took me all day to prepare.

And what happened when they were served? He flew into a rage and kicked the table over!

That was it! Enough!

"I resign!" I said.

"Good!" said the General. "No more garlic!"

The next day, the General's master of the household came to see me. "You're both great men," he said to me. "You deserve to be the General's chef, and he deserves the cooking of the greatest chef in all of France – you. A little give and take is all it needs, a little give and take…"

Finally he persuaded me to stay. So that night, as a peace offering, I cooked one of the General's favourite dishes: plain roast chicken, no garlic. Bah! But as the master of the household had said: "A little give and take…"

"The greatest chef in all of France"

At the end of the meal, the General called for me again. And he reached out and gave me a pat on the cheek, and grinned at me just as if we were the oldest of friends.

...if there had been such a magazine...

But even at times of peace, Napoleon always had enemies who were plotting, trying to make trouble – in particular Britain. The British government was always trying to persuade other countries to join them in a war against France. And it was always ready to give money and encouragement to royalist groups inside and outside France who wanted to make trouble. It was always ready to help anyone who had a plot to...

Chapter 6

Kill Napoleon

Sometimes something really small – like one glass of wine too many, or a fancy scarf – can change the course of history.

It was Christmas Eve. There was to be the first performance of Hayden's great oratorio *The Creation* that night at the Paris Opera House. Josephine, Napoleon's wife, and Hortense, his step-daughter, wanted to go. Napoleon, who'd had a hard day (as usual) didn't. He wanted to rest in front of a log fire at home, not go out in the cold. Eventually, Josephine managed to persuade him to come with them: "It'll do you good," she said.

As usual, the family were to travel in two coaches: Napoleon in the front coach; Josephine, Hortense and some friends in the second. As they were about to get into the coaches, Josephine stopped to rearrange her scarf. Napoleon, impatient as always, told his coachman to drive on.

They drove across the square in front of the palace towards the narrow street that led to the Opera.

Partly blocking the street was a horse and cart. On the cart was a large beer barrel. In the darkness, no-one noticed a man on the cart strike a flint, then jump from the cart and run away as fast as he could.

As it was Christmas Eve, César, Napoleon's coachman, had been celebrating with some of the other servants. Maybe he thought he was going to have the night off. He was usually a careful driver, but a couple of glasses of wine made him bold.

Instead of slowing down or stopping at the obstruction, César drove the horses through the narrow gap between the cart and the wall at top speed and into the street beyond. That may have saved Napoleon's life, because as the coach sped down the street the gunpowder packed into the barrel on the cart behind them exploded.

If the second carriage had been right behind, it would have been blown to smithereens. But because Josephine had been delayed, fiddling with her scarf, her carriage was still some distance away from the cart when it blew up, so she and Hortense and the rest of their party escaped with just a few cuts and bruises. But the people in the houses nearby weren't so lucky. The huge explosion ripped through the houses and nine people were killed.

Napoleon may have been the dictator of France, but the assassination plots showed him how vulnerable he was. Most kings and emperors weren't as powerful as he was, but when a king or emperor died there was never a gap. The very second they died a new king or emperor was created in their place. It was the ancient cry: "the king is dead – long live the king!" But when Napoleon died, there would be no-one to take his place.

Napoleon decided that the only thing he could do to protect France and the Empire was to make himself an emperor, just like the Emperor of Austria or the Tsar of Russia. That meant that when he died, his title of Emperor would be passed on to his heir – a son, if he had one, a brother if he didn't. Even if Napoleon was dead, France would still have a ruler: the next emperor.

Emperor

Beethoven, the great German composer, was a big fan of Napoleon. Even though Napoleon was French and Beethoven was German, Beethoven had wanted Napoleon to win the wars against Austria and Prussia. This was because Napoleon had promised to get rid of feudalism and all the old, unfair laws in a lot of Germany. Like Napoleon, Beethoven was a passionate believer in the ideals of the French Revolution.

Beethoven had just finished writing a new symphony. It was the largest, grandest, most revolutionary symphony ever written. He was going to call it *The Napoleon Symphony*, in honour of his hero. It was all ready, the dedication had even been written on the title page of the manuscript.

There was a knock at the door. A friend had arrived at Beethoven's house to tell him the astonishing news: "Napoleon has crowned himself Emperor."

At first, Beethoven refused to believe it. Then he flew into a dreadful rage, seized his pen, and with vicious gouges of the nib – as if he wanted to stab the Emperor himself – Beethoven scored out both the dedication and the title.

All over Europe, supporters reacted to the news in the same way as Beethoven – with disbelief, disgust and anger. It wasn't just disappointment; they felt betrayed.

Invade England!

But if Napoleon had been expecting a new respect from his fellow monarchs now that he was an emperor, he was mistaken. They were livid! They didn't see him as an emperor at all, they thought he was an imitation – "upstart" they called him.

And Britain was causing trouble again. The British government was once again at war with France and looking for allies. In 1805, Britain formed a new coalition with Russia and Prussia. Napoleon knew there could be no peace while Britain and her navy were free. Napoleon decided that the only solution was to invade England.

Secretly, Napoleon began to build ships and get an army together. By the early autumn of 1805, there were 100,000

French troops and 2,000 ships near the channel port of Bolougne ready to invade. But, first, the British navy, which was protecting the English coast, had to be got out of the way.

Napoleon's plan was simple: cause a diversion; lure the English ships away from the coast and into the open sea and leave the way clear for the invasion.

Putting together the finest ships from both the French and Spanish navies Napoleon ordered his ships to sail – not across the channel but in the opposite direction. The plan seemed to be working, the English navy followed. They chased the French and Spanish ships round the coast of France, south into the Atlantic Ocean.

Battle of Trafalgar

And that's where Napoleon's plan went horribly wrong. The English caught up with the French and Spanish fleet, near a cape on the coast of southern Spain called Trafalgar. Although the English commander, Admiral Nelson, was killed during the battle, the French and Spanish fleet was totally destroyed.

Napoleon had not only failed to destroy the English navy, but now he hadn't enough ships left to take his soldiers across the channel. The invasion of England had to be called off... again.

A European Empire

But things were very different for Napoleon on land. Literally turning his back on England, Napoleon marched his army from Bolougne into the middle of Europe to fight his other enemies: Russia, Prussia and Austria. On land he had his three greatest victories yet, the first of them just two months after the defeat at Trafalgar.

EUROPEAN CUP 1805–1807

FRANCE vs REST OF EUROPE

... **FIRST ROUND: Austerlitz, December 2, 1805...** 68,000 French troops, under the command of the Emperor, defeats 90,000 troops from both Russia and Austria... Enemy trapped on Pratzen Plane, 15,000 killed & 11,000 captured...

SECOND ROUND: Jena, October 14, 1806... 122,000 French troops, commanded by Napoleon, destroy the Prussian army...

THIRD ROUND: Friedland, June 14, 1807... Crushing defeat for Russians from French army, commanded by Napoleon.

Once again, Napoleon's victories had brought peace and new territories for the Empire. But Napoleon knew that the war wasn't over, it was just another truce; the Final was still to be played.

The Secrets of Napoleon's Success

The "secrets" of Napoleon's military success didn't change much over the years. They were:

- break the rules of war
- fight to win
- keep your soldiers under control – if you can't control them before or after a battle (looting, stealing etc.) you won't be able to control them during a battle and the ordinary civilians – who you are probably saving from the enemy – will hate you
- try to make things better for the citizens after you've conquered their country than they were before. Give them the good things from the revolution, such as no more feudalism, and fair laws and taxes
- don't turn your back on them – leave somebody you trust in charge to run things after you leave – preferably a member of your immediate family or one of your best friends

Being Part of the Empire

Napoleon didn't rule the whole Empire himself from Paris.
When he either conquered a new territory or was given it as
part of a peace treaty, he got rid of the old rulers and set up a
new state which had many of the good things of the French
system. And when he got rid of the old rulers, he often
replaced them with either members of his family or his
closest friends.

Napoleon's dream was to rule an Empire where the laws
were fair to everyone, there were no special privileges for
nobles or clergy, the citizens of each country elected their
own parliaments and everyone could follow the religion of
their choice.

What stopped his dream from coming true were the
constant wars. To pay for the wars, Napoleon had to raise very
heavy taxes and force young men from all over the Empire into
the army.

So despite all the good things the Empire gave them, the people of Westphalia, Italy, Holland and the rest hated the Empire because of the high taxes and their young men being forced to fight in the French army.

Napoleon decided to try and stop the wars once and for all. He knew that another huge war was inevitable, but this time he would try and utterly destroy one of his most powerful enemies before they had a chance to attack him first. He'd never lost a battle on land, so he was confident that he could win such an enormous victory that no-one would ever dare to threaten him again.

He decided to invade Russia.

War in a Wasteland

Napoleon gathered troops from all the Empire into what he called The Grand Army. In June 1812 he led 650,000 soldiers into Russia.

The Russian army's tactics were brilliant. The Russian army retreated. They refused to fight, and Napoleon and his army were led deeper and deeper into Russia without having once fought a battle. As the Russian troops retreated, they burnt all the towns and the crops as they went. Napoleon's army found only scorched earth.

Because Russia is so vast, and so far from France, it was impossible for the Grand Army to be supplied with food and other provisions from France. Napoleon had been relying on "foraging" – stealing – most of what the army needed. But the Russian troops left nothing behind: no food, no shelter.

The French army reached Moscow in September, exhausted and hungry. Napoleon had been planning for the army to spend the winter in Moscow, and continue the invasion in the spring.

Moscow was the first city or large town the French had come to which hadn't already been destroyed. But once again, most of the people had vanished. Only a few hard-looking men lurked in the shadows of the buildings.

The first night the Grand Army spent in Moscow fires suddenly broke out all over the city. Napoleon's men searched desperately for hoses and pumps to put out the fires. They'd all been removed. They tried to fight the fires with buckets, but it was no good. A strong wind spread the fires from house to

house and from street to street. As Napoleon and his officers watched helplessly, the city of Moscow burned around them.

Napoleon turned his army round and started to retreat back to France. But winter had started, and the snow was falling fast. Suddenly Russian troops were everywhere, attacking the long line of exhausted, freezing French troops. Thousands froze to death in the snow, or died of starvation.

Of the Grand Army of 650,000 men who had crossed the border in June, only 40,000 got back to France.

Chapter 7

The End
of the Empire

This was the moment Napoleon's enemies had been waiting for. Napoleon had been defeated and lost most of his army. They attacked from all directions. The Russian army attacked France from the east, Prussia from the north, and the British army invaded Spain and attacked from the south.

In 1810, Napoleon had divorced the Empress Josephine, who hadn't given him an heir, and married Marie Louise, the daughter of the Emperor of Austria. He was sure his own father-in-law wouldn't attack him; he was wrong.

Paris was surrounded and surrendered. Napoleon was taken prisoner. Under the terms of the peace treaty, Napoleon was banished to the tiny island of Elba in the Mediterranean.

As he was about to board the ship to leave France for Elba, he was surrounded by his old comrades – the Old Guard who had fought under him all over Europe. He turned to them and made this speech:

" Soldiers of my Old Guard, I bid you good-bye. For twenty years I have found you uninterruptedly on the path of honour and glory. Lately no less than when things went well you have been models of courage and loyalty. With men like you our cause was not lost; but the war could not be ended: it would have been civil war, and that would only have brought France more misfortune. So I have sacrificed our interests to those of our homeland; I am leaving; you, my friends, are going to go on serving France. France's happiness was my one thought; and it will always be what I wish for most. Don't be sorry for me; if I have chosen to go on living, I have done so in order to go on serving your glory. I want to write about the great things we have done together! . . . Goodbye, my children! I should like to press you all to my heart; at least I shall kiss your flag! . . . "

What a speech; what a performance! Everyone was in tears, including some of the British, Austrian and Prussian troops who were waiting to take the captured emperor into exile.

Today if a famous leader went into exile, journalists from all around the world would be clamouring for an exclusive interview. Let's just imagine that an intrepid reporter braved the journey to the island of Elba and returned with this scoop . . .

NAPOLEON:
THE Celebrity Questionnnaire

Q What's your favourite place?

A Corsica – where I was born.

Q What was your favourite subject at school?

A Mathematics.

Q What was your least favourite?

A Spelling and handwriting – oh, and dancing, too. I was always a terrible speller and a dreadful dancer.

Q What's your favourite food?

A Plain food – vegetables, potatoes, beans. I once had a dish invented specially for me: Chicken Morengo, named after my victory in the war against the Austrians. It was made up from a few ingredients – a chicken, tomatoes, a couple of crayfish – which my cook managed to find after the battle. Rather like your "Ready, Steady, Cook".

Q What's your favourite word?

A Three words: Freedom, Equality, Brotherhood.

Q Meaning...?

A It's the slogan of the Revolution. It means freedom for everyone from poverty and injustice, and from unfair laws. It means everyone is equal under the law – not different laws for the rich and for the poor. It means all men are brothers – no-one is born to rule over or own anyone else.

Q Who was the love of your life?

A France.

Q No, I mean a person.

A The Empress Josephine ... and my son.

Q But you divorced Josephine in 1810 and married the daughter of the Austrian Emperor.

A But that was for France. Josephine could not give me an heir. Without an heir the Empire would collapse after I was dead.

Q It collapsed anyway, even though you had an heir.

A Yes, I know.

Q What qualities do you most dislike in other people?

A Extravagance – a love of luxuries and expensive toys and clothes – and dishonesty. I particularly hate the dishonesty of politicians such as Talleyrand and Metternich.

Q What quality do you most dislike in yourself?

A Impatience. Maybe if I had been more patient, and we'd wintered in Moscow, I would not have lost the Grand Army. But then if I had been patient and waited in Egypt, I would never have become Consul and Emperor.

Q What qualities do you think others most admire in you?

A Firstly, energy. I can work all day and all night, and just take the odd nap when I want. Some people have said I must have exceptionally large lungs to have so much energy! And my memory. I can remember the faces and names of my soldiers years after the battles they fought in; and I can remember maps after just a quick glance.

Q What do you most regret?

A That I could never bring peace to the Empire so that everybody could enjoy the benefits of freedom, good laws and prosperity.

Q Who do you blame for that?

A The English!

One Last Try

Louis XVI's brother came back to rule as king Louis XVIII. (Louis XVII, Louis XVI's son, had died in prison just a few years after his father's execution.)

The nobles who had been living abroad came back. The new government was determined to get rid of all traces of the revolution. All the old privileges were brought back. The ordinary people hated the return to the old ways. They'd got used to living without lords telling them what to do and robbing them.

Throughout France people were saying: "Things were better under Napoleon. I wish the emperor would come back." It didn't take long for word to reach the King of Elba.

Napoleon slipped away from Elba secretly and landed in Marseilles in March 1815, with just a handful of men. He'd promised himself that if a single shot was fired against him, he would turn round and go back rather than have to fight a fellow Frenchman. He didn't have to worry. Everywhere he went, people yelled: "Long live the emperor!" As he marched north to Paris, more and more ex-soldiers joined him. The king fled. By June, Napoleon had an army of 72,000 men. But the countries against him – Austria, Britain, Russia and Prussia –

La Soleil says:

Life was better under Boney!

Toodle-oo, Louis!

Bring Back Napoleon!

Long Live the Emperor!

See page 3 for exclusive pics of Josephine!

were putting together six armies totalling almost one million men.

The British army under the command of the Duke of Wellington had already invaded Belgium and was waiting for Napoleon, but the two Prussian armies hadn't marched so fast and hadn't linked up with the British. This was just the situation which Napoleon liked best – attacking his enemies before they were ready. On June 16th, Napoleon launched one of his surprise attacks on one of the Prussian armies, which was still several kilometres from the British army. He won. But on June 18th he attacked the British army near a small town in Belgium called Waterloo.

Napoleon's Waterloo

The battle began in the early morning. Although the weather was fine, rain had been falling heavily for several days and the ground was very muddy. Napoleon decided not to attack Wellington's main army until midday, to let the ground dry out a little. This was a fatal mistake. As Wellington admitted, if Napoleon had attacked early he would have won. By delaying, Napoleon gave the second Prussian army enough time to reach Waterloo. When Napoleon's troops finally attacked, they

were now fighting two armies instead of one. Napoleon's army was outnumbered and defeated. But it could so easily have been another victory for Napoleon. The next day, Wellington called the Battle of Waterloo: "The nearest-run thing you ever saw in your life".

The prisoner of St Helena

Napoleon knew that if he was captured by the Prussians they would execute him. He rode away from the battlefield and returned to Paris. From Paris he went to the port of Rochefort, where there was a British ship anchored, the *Bellerephon*. He surrendered to the Captain, on the understanding that he would be taken to Britain.

But the British government didn't want him to come to Britain. Instead, the *Bellerephon* was ordered to take Napoleon to the tiny island of St Helena in the South Atlantic Ocean, 1834 kilometres from the coast of Africa and 8046 kilometres from France. Realising he had been double-crossed, Napoleon wrote a letter to the British government. This is part of it:

I hearby solemnly protest against this injustice... I came freely on board the "Bellerephon". I am not a prisoner. I am the guest of England... I gave myself up in good faith and claimed the protection of the English laws. If I am exiled to St Helena, it will impossible for the English to talk about their good name, their laws and their liberty. British good faith will have been lost... I appeal to history.

But Napoleon's appeal was ignored. Napoleon was kept prisoner on St Helena, guarded by a garrison of almost 2,000 British troops until 1821, when he died of stomach cancer at the age of 51.

Not the End

People die, but ideas have ways of living on.

In 1830 and 1848, revolutions started all over Europe. People in Italy, Germany and France hadn't forgotten what it had been like to have a country of their own under Napoleon's Empire. But this time, they promised themselves, it would be their own country, not ruled by a foreign lord or prince or Emperor. It was what Carlo Bonaparte and Pasquale Paoli had wanted for Corsica before Napoleon was born.

France didn't forget Napoleon's reforms, either. French laws are still based on the code Napoleon drew up.

And no-one in Europe could forget the French Revolution and its ideals: Freedom, Equality and Brotherhood. These ideas haunted the old emperors and kings, who desperately tried to go back to the old ways. But they couldn't work. The ordinary people remembered what it was like to be free of their lords and bishops. One day, they would elect rulers who would govern in the interests of the ordinary people.

One day there would be Freedom, Equality and Brotherhood for all!

Lifeline

1769 Napoleon is born in Corsica

1796 He marries Josephine de Beauharnais

1799 Napoleon seizes power in France

1804 He crowns himself Emperor of the French people

1805 He defeats his enemies at Austerlitz

1810 He marries Marie Louise of Austria

1812 Napoleon enters Moscow

1814 Napoleon is exiled on Elba

1815 He is defeated at the Battle of Waterloo

1821 Napoleon dies on the island of St Helena

titles in the series

Spilling the Beans on Julius Caesar

Spilling the Beans on Einstein

Spilling the Beans on Tutankhamen

Spilling the Beans on Shakespeare

Spilling the Beans on Robin Hood

Spilling the Beans on Napoleon

Spilling the Beans on Buffalo Bill

Spilling the Beans on Marie Antoinette

Spilling the Beans on Joan of Arc

Spilling the Beans on Boudicca

Spilling the Beans on Darwin

Spilling the Beans on Blackbeard

Spilling the Beans on Making it in Football

Spilling the Beans on Making it in The Ballet

Spilling the Beans on Making it in The Movies

Spilling the Beans on Making it in Music

Spilling the Beans on Making it in Computers

Spilling the Beans on Making it in Fashion